Especially for

_____

From

_____

Date

© 2011 by Barbour Publishing, Inc.

Written and compiled by Ellyn Sanna.

ISBN 978-1-61626-321-8

Scripture quotations marked CEV are from the Contemporary English Version, Copyright © 1991, 1992, 1995 by American Bible Society, Used by permission.

Scripture quotations marked MSG are taken from THE MESSAGE. Copyright © by Eugene H. Peterson 1993, 1994, 1995, 1996, 2000, 2001, 2002. Used by permission of NavPress Publishing Group.

Scripture quotations marked NCV are taken from the New Century Version of the Bible. Copyright © 2005 by Thomas Nelson, Inc. Used by permission.

Scripture quotations marked NIV are taken from the HOLY BIBLE, NEW INTERNATIONAL VERSION®, NIV®. Copyright 1973, 1978, 1984, 2010 by Biblica, Inc.™ Used by permission. All rights reserved worldwide.

Scripture quotations marked NLT are taken from the Holy Bible, New Living Translation. Copyright © 1996, 2004. Used by permission of Tyndale House Publishers, Wheaton, Illinois 60189. All rights reserved.

Scripture quotations marked NASB are taken from the New American Standard Bible, © 1960, 1962, 1963, 1968, 1971, 1972, 1973, 1975, 1995 by The Lockman Foundation. Used by permission.

Scripture quotations marked KJV are taken from the King James Version of the Bible.

Published by Barbour Publishing, Inc., P.O. Box 719, Uhrichsville, Ohio 44683, www.barbourbooks.com

Our mission is to publish and distribute inspirational products offering exceptional value and biblical encouragement to tme masses.

Member of the
Evangelical Christian
Publishers Association

Printed in China.

power
of
love

BARBOUR
PUBLISHING

Introduction

Everyone needs love; everyone
talks about love; everyone wants
love. But not everyone knows
what love truly means.

Contrary to common belief,
possessiveness is not love. Nor
is jealousy love, and neither is fear.
Keeping people all to yourself is not love.
Expecting something from someone is not love.

Instead, real love is unconditional. It gives of
itself no matter what. The greatest thinkers down
through the centuries have known this and shared
with us their wisdom in their writing.

Ultimately, real love is what Jesus showed to us
on the cross. And God is love. Where love exists,
there God is present.

Love. . .puts up with anything,
Trusts God always,
Always looks for the best,
Never looks back,
But keeps going to the end.
Love never dies.

1 Corinthians 13:4, 7–8 MSG

Love is hard work. It asks us to be our best selves, to keep striving to be more, to do better, to go against our natural inclinations, and to put the other first.

And because we are loved in return, we know that our worst selves are accepted, that our failures are forgiven, and that our needs are respected.

To love, and to be loved,
is the greatest happiness of existence.

SYDNEY SMITH

• • • • •

It is a gift of God to be able to
share our love with others.

MOTHER TERESA

• • • • •

Love has its source in God,
for love is the very essence of His being.

KAY ARTHUR

If you had no one to love, you would never be hurt but you would never grow. You would never venture outside your own self-centered needs and perceptions. Your heart would never be cracked open so that God could enter it.

God reveals Himself to us through human love.

Doubting the reality of love
leads to doubting everything.

HENRI-FRÉDÉRIC AMIEL

• • • • •

Love is not getting, but giving. . . .
It is goodness and honor and peace and pure
living. Yes, love is that and it is the best thing in
the world and the thing that lives the longest.

HENRY VAN DYKE

We so easily forget what is most important. What does it really matter if my bank account is nearly empty, if I'm embarrassed by a professional mistake, or if I've gained ten pounds? If the people I love are healthy and happy, what more do I really need?

Love gives the rest of life its meaning. Without it, life is empty. With it, life is full and overflowing.

A loving heart is the truest wisdom.

CHARLES DICKENS

• • • • •

In the presence of love, miracles happen!

ROBERT SCHULLER

• • • • •

Love is not blind; it is an extra eye,
which shows us what is most worthy of regard.

JAMES MATTHEW BARRIE

Because I love you, I catch glimpses of the "you" God created, the true you. I see your imperfections and failures, but I choose to see past them to the real you.

Love creates a place where you are free to become your complete self.

We are all born for love. It is the principle
of existence and its only end.

BENJAMIN DISRAELI

• • • • •

Love is a debt which inclination
always pays, obligation never.

BLAISE PASCAL

• • • • •

Love accomplishes all things.

PETRARCH

"*All people will know that you are my followers if you love each other.*"

JOHN 13:35 NCV

Love isn't a pretty feeling that floats around the world. It's tough and practical and active. Love is washing the kitchen floor over and over and over. It's scrubbing the toilet and doing the laundry. Love is taking out the garbage and cleaning the refrigerator. It's smiling when you're tired and finding reasons to laugh even when you're angry. Love is taking the dirty job, lightening the other's load, lending a hand. Love goes out of its way to be kind. Love takes a stand. Love works hard and makes the world a better place.

Love sought is good,
but given unsought is better.

WILLIAM SHAKESPEARE

• • • • •

Love remembers everything.

OVID

• • • • •

Just as a flower gives out its fragrance to anyone
who approaches or uses it, so love from within
us radiates toward everybody and manifests
as spontaneous service.

RAMDAS

God says to us, "In love, I hold you in My mind. I remember you. I hold all the pieces of you, the past ones and the present, and in love, I knit them together into the person I love, the person I created to give Me joy: you!"

We do not need to earn God's love. It is ours simply because we are who we are and He is who He is.

The pleasure of love is in loving.
We are happier in the passion we feel
than in that we inspire.

FRANÇOIS DE LA ROCHEFOUCAULD

• • • • •

One word frees us of all the weight
and pain of life; that word is love.

SOPHOCLES

Real love is not wanting or needing something from another person. Real love is giving whatever we have to give and being content even to give nothing when nothing is needed that we have to offer. True love makes us invisible to ourselves. It sees only the other person, seeks only that person's good, no matter the cost. Love is never easy. And yet love lightens all life's hardest burdens.

Life is a flower of which love is the honey.

VICTOR HUGO

• • • • •

Love is the beginning, the middle,
and the end of everything.

JEAN B. H. LACORDAIRE

God created the world from love. It is knit into the very cells of our bodies. It is written into our DNA; and it is spelled out in the chemicals that make plants green, the sky blue, and human flesh its many variations of brown, pink, and tan. It is the song birds sing on summer mornings, the whisper of the wind in the trees, and the silence of snow falling. It is God's voice calling to us endlessly through all creation.

Pure love is matchless in majesty;
it has no parallel in power and there
is no darkness it cannot dispel.

MEHER BABA

• • • • •

Love doesn't make the world go 'round.
Love is what makes the ride worthwhile.

FRANKLIN P. JONES

One must learn to love. . .and the journey
is always toward the other soul.

D. H. LAWRENCE

• • • • •

To love is to place our happiness
in the happiness of another.

GOTTFRIED WILHELM VON LEIBNIZ

• • • • •

Give all to love.
Obey thy heart.

RALPH WALDO EMERSON

Love is the only thing that we can carry with us
when we go, and it makes the end so easy.

LOUISA MAY ALCOTT

• • • • •

Love is life, love is the lamp that lights the
universe: without that light this goodly frame,
the earth, is a barren promontory
and man the quintessence of dust.

MARY ELIZABETH BRADDON

Love and the gentle heart
are but a single thing.

DANTE ALIGHIERI

• • • • •

When love and skill work together,
expect a masterpiece.

JOHN RUSKIN

• • • • •

Between whom there is hearty truth,
there is love.

HENRY DAVID THOREAU

There is no fear in love.
But perfect love drives out fear.
1 JOHN 4:18 NIV

• • • • •

God is love.
Whoever lives in love lives in God,
and God in them. . . .
Love is made complete among us.
1 JOHN 4:16–17 NIV

Take away love and our earth is a tomb.

ROBERT BROWNING

• • • • •

Any time that is not spent on love is wasted.

TORQUATO TASSO

• • • • •

If you wish to be loved, love.

LUCIUS ANNAEUS SENECA

The best proof of love is trust.

JOYCE BROTHERS

Love doesn't just sit there, like a stone,
it has to be made, like bread;
remade all the time, made new.

URSULA LE GUIN

• • • • •

Love will find its way
Thro' paths where wolves would fear to prey.

GEORGE GORDON BYRON

• • • • •

Love is all we have, the only way
that each can help the other.

EURIPIDES

Love is but the discovery
of ourselves in others,
and the delight in the recognition.

Alexander Smith

True love's the gift which God has given
To man alone beneath the heaven
It is the secret sympathy,
The silver link, the silken tie,
Which heart to heart, and mind to mind,
In body and in soul can bind.

SIR WALTER SCOTT

Love. . .is to build a house with affection,
even as if your beloved were to dwell in that house.
It is to sow seeds with tenderness and reap with
joy, even as if your beloved were to eat the fruit.

KHALIL GIBRAN

• • • • • • •

But true love is a durable fire
In the mind ever burning;
Never sick, never old, never dead,
From itself never turning.

WALTER RALEIGH

The heart that loves is always young.

GREEK PROVERB

• • • • •

Love is a great beautifier.

LOUISA MAY ALCOTT

• • • • •

I always think that the best way
to know God is to love many things.

VINCENT VAN GOGH

The beginning of love is to let
those we love be perfectly themselves,
and not to twist them to fit our own image.
Otherwise, we love only the reflection
of ourselves we find in them.

THOMAS MERTON

• • • • •

We need in love to practice only this:
letting each other go.
For holding on comes easily;
we do not need to learn it.

RAINER MARIA RILKE

Where love is concerned,
too much is not even enough.

PIERRE-AUGUSTIN DE BEAUMARCHAIS

• • • • •

Love seeks not to possess,
but to be possessed.

R. H. BENSON

• • • • •

To love another you have to undertake
some fragment of their destiny.

QUENTIN CRISP

I hold this to be the highest task
for a bond between two people,
that each protects the solitude
of the other.

RAINER MARIA RILKE

There is no difficulty that enough love will not conquer; no disease that enough love will not heal; no door that enough love will not open; no gulf that enough love will not bridge; no wall that enough love will not throw down; no sin that enough love will not redeem. . . . It makes no difference how deeply seated may be the trouble; how hopeless the outlook; how muddled the tangle; how great the mistake. A sufficient realization of love will dissolve it all. If only you could love enough, you would be the happiest and most powerful being in the world.

EMMET FOX

*I led them with kindness
and with love, not with ropes.
I held them close to me;
I bent down to feed them.*

HOSEA 11:4 CEV

• • • • •

Let all that you do be done in love.

1 CORINTHIANS 16:14 NASB

Take hold lightly; let go lightly.
This is one of the great secrets of felicity in love.

SPANISH PROVERB

· · · · ·

Love cures people—both the ones who give it
and the ones who receive it.

KARL MENNINGER

· · · · ·

Love conquers all things.

VIRGIL

It is the special quality of love not to be able to remain stationary, to be obliged to increase under pain of diminishing.

ANDRÉ GIDE

• • • • •

I believe in the sun even if it isn't shining.
I believe in love even when I am alone.
I believe in God even when He is silent.

UNKNOWN

The courage to share
your feelings is critical to
sustaining a love relationship.
HAROLD H. BLOOMFIELD

Love is the wisdom of the fool
and the folly of the wise.
SAMUEL JOHNSON

• • • • •

When one has once fully entered
the realm of love, the world—
no matter how imperfect—
becomes rich and beautiful,
it consists solely of
opportunities for love.
SØREN KIERKEGAARD

Love is. . .an endless mystery,
for it has nothing else to explain it.

Rabindranath Tagore

• • • • •

We find rest in those we love, and we provide a
resting place in ourselves for those who love us.

Bernard of Clairvaux

• • • • •

Love knows no laws.

Sir John Lyly

It is love, not reason, that is stronger than death.
THOMAS MANN

• • • • •

To love someone is to see
a miracle invisible to others.
FRANÇOIS MAURIAC

• • • • •

If you love somebody, tell them.
ROD MCKUEN

Love is. . .the force that joins to good
and joins us to the world through good.
Its existence is the unmistakable sign that
we are spiritual creatures,
attracted by excellence and made for the good.
It is a reflection of the warmth and light of the sun.

IRIS MURDOCH

• • • • •

And what is it to work with love?
It is to weave the cloth with threads drawn
from your heart, even as if your beloved were
to wear that cloth.

KHALIL GIBRAN

If you have love in your life,
it can make up for a great many things
that are missing. If you don't have
love in your life, no matter what else
there is, it's not enough.

Ann Landers

Love is patient and kind. Love is not jealous,
it does not brag, and it is not proud.

1 CORINTHIANS 13:4 NCV

There is a way from your heart to mine.
And my heart knows it.

RUMI

• • • • •

You are the kernel of my heart,
You are the face of my sun,
You are the harp of my music,
You are the crown of my company.

CELTIC BLESSING

The heart has its reasons
which reason does not understand.

BLAISE PASCAL

• • • • •

At the touch of love
everyone becomes a poet.

PLATO

• • • • •

Love is space and time made
directly perceptible to the heart.

MARCEL PROUST

I carry your heart. . .in my heart.

E. E. CUMMINGS

• • • • •

Love was for me a delicate thread stretched
between two adjacent pegs, but now it has
been transformed into a halo; its first is its last,
and its last is its first. It encompasses
every being, slowly expanding to
embrace all that will ever be.

RUMI

For one human being to love another:
that is perhaps the most difficult of our tasks;
the ultimate, the last test and proof, the work for
which all other work is but preparation.

RAINER MARIA RILKE

•   •   •   •   •

If we deny love that is given to us, if we refuse to
give love because we fear pain or loss,
then our lives will be empty, our loss greater.

FRANÇOIS DE LA ROCHEFOUCAULD

Among those whom I like or admire,
I can find no common denominator,
but among those whom I love,
I can: all of them make me laugh.

W. H. AUDEN

• • • • •

Sometimes it's a form of love just to talk to
somebody that you have nothing in common
with and still be fascinated by their presence.

DAVID BYRNE

Love is like the moon;
when it does not increase, it decreases.

SEGUR

• • • • •

Love sees with the heart and not the mind.

WILLIAM SHAKESPEARE

• • • • •

We love the things we love for what they are.

ROBERT FROST

To love for the sake of being
loved is human;
but to love for the sake
of loving is angelic.
ALPHONSE DE LAMARTINE

• • • • •

Love is the greatest refreshment of life.
PABLO PICASSO

Love is indestructible,
Its holy flame forever burneth;
From heaven it came,
to heaven returneth.
It soweth here with toil and care,
But the harvest time of love is there.

ROBERT SOUTHEY

Immature love says:
"I love you because I need you."
Mature love says:
"I need you because I love you."

ERIC FROMME

• • • • •

"Love" is supreme and unconditional;
"like" is nice but limited.

DUKE ELLINGTON

It is best to love wisely, no doubt;
but to love foolishly is better than
not to be able to love at all.

WILLIAM MAKEPEACE THACKERAY

• • • • •

The first duty of love is to listen.

PAUL TILLICH

• • • • •

Love is an act of endless forgiveness,
a tender look which becomes a habit.

PETER USTINOV

There is but one genuine love potion—
consideration.

MENANDER

• • • • •

To love deeply in one direction
makes us more loving in all others.

MADAME SWETCHINE

• • • • •

How vast a memory has Love!

ALEXANDER POPE

The most wonderful of all things in life,
I believe, is the discovery of another
human being with whom one's relationship
has a glowing depth, beauty, and joy as the
years increase. This inner progressiveness
of love between two human beings is a most
marvelous thing, it cannot be found by looking
for it or by passionately wishing for it.
It is a sort of divine accident.

SIR HUGH WALPOLE

To love is to receive

a glimpse of heaven.

KAREN SUNDE

Let us not love with words or speech
but with actions and in truth.
1 JOHN 3:18 NIV

• • • • •

Many waters cannot quench love,
neither can the floods drown it.
SONG OF SOLOMON 8:7 KJV

Whether love is from heaven or earth,
it points to God.

RUMI

• • • • •

Love overflows into all:
From the glorious ocean depths
to beyond the farthest star.

HILDEGARD VON BINGEN

• • • • •

Love is a canvas furnished by nature
and embroidered by imagination.

VOLTAIRE

The art of love. . .is largely
the art of persistence.

ALBERT ELLIS

• • • • •

In so far as love is a union,
it knows no extremes of distance.

JUANA INÉS DE LA CRUZ

Life has taught us that love
does not consist in gazing at each other
but in looking outward in the same direction.

ANTOINE DE SAINT-EXUPÉRY

• • • • • •

Gratitude looks to the past,
and love to the present.

C. S. LEWIS

There is no surprise more magical
than the surprise of being loved.
It is God's finger on man's shoulder.

Charles Morgan

• • • • •

Time is too slow for those who wait,
too swift for those who fear,
too long for those who grieve,
too short for those who rejoice,
but for those who love,
time is eternity.

Henry van Dyke

Love has no desire but to fulfill itself.
To melt and be like a running brook
that sings its melody to the night.
To wake at dawn with a winged heart
and give thanks for another day of loving.

KHALIL GIBRAN

• • • • •

Love is a symbol of eternity. It wipes out
all sense of time, destroying all memory
of a beginning and all fear of an end.

UNKNOWN

Who, being loved, is poor?

OSCAR WILDE

•   •   •   •   •

Love must be as much a light,
as it is a flame.

HENRY DAVID THOREAU

•   •   •   •   •

Love is the condition in which the happiness of
another person is essential to your own.

ROBERT HEINLEIN

The past is behind us,
love is in front and all around us.

TERRI GUILLEMETS

• • • • •

Such ever was love's way:
to rise, it stoops.

ROBERT BROWNING

You don't have to go looking for love when it's where you come from.

WERNER ERHARD

Love unlocks doors and opens windows
that weren't even there before.
MIGNON McLAUGHLIN

• • • • •

'Tis better to have loved and lost
than never to have loved at all.
ALFRED, LORD TENNYSON

Without love, the rich and poor live
in the same house.

UNKNOWN

. . . . .

Loving is never a waste of time.

ASTRID ALAUDA

. . . . .

Love is not consolation. It is light.

FRIEDRICH NIETZSCHE

The arms of love encompass you
with your present, your past, your future,
the arms of love gather you together.

ANTOINE DE SAINT-EXUPÉRY

• • • • •

The supreme happiness of life is the conviction
that we are loved; loved for ourselves, or rather,
loved in spite of ourselves.

VICTOR HUGO

You can give without loving,
but you can never love without giving.
UNKNOWN

• • • • •

Love is not blind—it sees more, not less.
JULIUS GORDON

• • • • •

Nothing is too much trouble for love.
DESMOND TUTU

True love is when you put someone
on a pedestal and they fall,
but you are there to catch them.

UNKNOWN

• • • • •

I love you as you are, not as you wish
to be. I love you for the real person
you are, not the imaginary person
I fantasize you could be. I love the
real, amazing, utterly unique you.

ANNA T. COBIN

As an act of love, prayer is a courageous act. It is a risk we take. It is a life-and-death risk, believing in the promises of the gospel, that God's love is indeed operative in the world. In prayer we have the courage, perhaps even the presumption and the arrogance or the audacity to claim that God's love can be operative in the very specific situations of human need that we encounter.

JOHN E. BIERSDORF

It is absolutely clear that God has called you to a free life. Just make sure that you don't use this freedom as an excuse to do whatever you want to do and destroy your freedom.
Rather, use your freedom to serve one another in love; that's how freedom grows. For everything we know about God's Word is summed up in a single sentence: Love others as you love yourself. That's an act of true freedom. If you bite and ravage each other, watch out— in no time at all you will be annihilating each other, and where will your precious freedom be then?

GALATIANS 5:13–15 MSG

A loving heart is the beginning
of all knowledge.

THOMAS CARLYLE

• • • • •

A man content to go to heaven alone
will never go to heaven.

BOETHIUS

• • • • •

Being deeply loved by someone gives you
strength, while loving someone
deeply gives you courage.

LAO TZU

Do all things with love.

OG MANDINO

• • • • •

I have found the paradox that
if you love until it hurts,
there can be no more hurt,
only more love.

MOTHER TERESA

• • • • •

Your task is not to seek love, but merely to
seek and find all the barriers within yourself
that you have built against love.

RUMI

If you judge people,
you have no time to love them.

MOTHER TERESA

• • • •

Life without love is like a tree
without blossoms or fruit.

KAHLIL GIBRAN

• • • •

Looking back, I have this to regret,
that too often when I loved, I did not say so.

DAVID GRAYSON

Love is the beauty of the soul.

SAINT AUGUSTINE

Nobody has ever measured, not even poets,
how much the heart can hold.

ZELDA FITZGERALD

• • • • •

Love takes up
where knowledge leaves off.

SAINT THOMAS AQUINAS

• • • • •

If love dwelt not in trouble,
it could have nothing to love.

JAKOB BOEHME

The hardest of all is learning to be
a well of affection, and not a fountain;
to show them we love them not when
we feel like it, but when they do.

NAN FAIRBROTHER

• • • • •

Love is not an affectionate feeling,
but a steady wish for the loved person's
ultimate good as far as it can be obtained.

C. S. LEWIS

You will find as you look back upon your life that the moments when you have truly lived are the moments when you have done things in the spirit of love.

HENRY DRUMMOND

• • • • •

A life lived in love will never be dull.

LEO BUSCAGLIA

Life is meaningless only if we allow it to be.
Each of us has the power to give life meaning,
to make our time and our bodies and our words
into instruments of love and hope.

TOM HEAD

• • • • •

Love many things, for therein lies the true
strength, and whosoever loves much performs
much, and can accomplish much,
and what is done in love is done well.

VINCENT VAN GOGH

The more I think it over, the more I feel
that there is nothing more truly artistic
than to love people.

VINCENT VAN GOGH

• • • • •

Love is a great thing,
yea, a great and thorough good;
by itself it makes everything that is heavy, light;
and it bears evenly all that is uneven.

THOMAS À KEMPIS

Your great love reaches to the skies,
your truth to the clouds.

PSALM 57:10 NCV

• • • • •

I'm absolutely convinced that nothing—
nothing living or dead, angelic or demonic,
today or tomorrow, high or low,
thinkable or unthinkable—absolutely nothing
can get between us and God's love
because of the way that Jesus
our Master has embraced us.

ROMANS 8:38–39 MSG

Love's greatest gift is its ability to make
everything it touches sacred.

Barbara De Angelis

• • • • •

We look forward to the time when the
power of love will replace the love of power.
Then will our world know the blessings of peace.

William E. Gladstone

Love and kindness are never wasted.

They always make a difference.

They bless the one who receives them,

and they bless you, the giver.

BARBARA DE ANGELIS

The one thing we can never get enough of is love. And the one thing we can never give enough of is love.

HENRY MILLER

Keep love in your heart.
A life without it is like a sunless
garden when the flowers are dead.
The consciousness of loving and being
loved brings a warmth and richness
to life that nothing else can bring.

OSCAR WILDE

We must develop and maintain the capacity
to forgive. He who is devoid of the power
to forgive is devoid of the power to love.
There is some good in the worst of us
and some evil in the best of us.
When we discover this,
we are less prone to hate our enemies.

MARTIN LUTHER KING JR.

• • • • •

Happiness is the spiritual experience of living
every minute with love, grace, and gratitude.

DENIS WAITLEY

We can only learn to love by loving.

IRIS MURDOCH

• • • • •

Love is more than just a feeling:
it's a process requiring continual attention.
Loving well takes laughter, loyalty,
and wanting more to be able to say,
"I understand" than to hear, "You're right."

MOLLEEN MATSUMURA

He is not a lover who does not love forever.

EURIPIDES

• • • • •

Where there is great love,
there are always miracles.

WILLA CATHER

• • • • •

I believe that unarmed truth and unconditional
love will have the final word in reality.

MARTIN LUTHER KING JR.

Although the act of nurturing another's spiritual growth has the effect of nurturing one's own, a major characteristic of genuine love is that the distinction between oneself and the other is always maintained and preserved.

M. Scott Peck

• • • • •

Love is never lost. If not reciprocated, it will flow back and soften and purify the heart.

Washington Irving

Love is more important than anything else.
It is what ties everything completely together.

COLOSSIANS 3:14 CEV

•   •   •   •   •

And this hope will never disappoint us,
because God has poured out his love to fill our
hearts. He gave us his love through the
Holy Spirit, whom God has given to us.

ROMANS 5:5 NCV

•   •   •   •   •

Hatred starts fights, but love pulls
a quilt over the bickering.

PROVERBS 10:12 MSG

If you were all alone in the universe with no one to talk to, no one with which to share the beauty of the stars, to laugh with, to touch, what would be your purpose in life? It is other life, it is love, which gives your life meaning. This is harmony. We must discover the joy of each other, the joy of challenge, the joy of growth.

MITSUGI SAOTOME

When we feel love and
kindness toward others,
it not only makes others feel
loved and cared for,
but it helps us also to develop
inner happiness and peace.

Tenzin Gyatso

While I'm locked up here, a prisoner for the Master, I want you to get out there and walk— better yet, run!—on the road God called you to travel. I don't want any of you sitting around on your hands. I don't want anyone strolling off, down some path that goes nowhere. And mark that you do this with humility and discipline—not in fits and starts, but steadily, pouring yourselves out for each other in acts of love, alert at noticing differences and quick at mending fences.

EPHESIANS 4:1–3 MSG

Nothing we do, however virtuous,
can be accomplished alone;
therefore, we are saved by love.
No virtuous act is quite as virtuous from the
standpoint of our friend or foe as from our own;
therefore, we are saved by the final form of love,
which is forgiveness.

REINHOLD NIEBUHR

Love, like truth and beauty, is concrete.
Love is not fundamentally a sweet feeling;
not, at heart, a matter of sentiment, attachment,
or being "drawn toward." Love is active,
effective, a matter of making reciprocal
and mutually beneficial relation with
one's friends and enemies.

CARTER HEYWARD

• • • • •

To love anyone is to hope in him always.

UNKNOWN

You learn to speak by speaking,
to study by studying, to run by running,
to work by working;
and just so, you learn to love by loving.

SAINT FRANCIS DE SALES

● ● ● ● ●

When we come into contact with the other
person, our thoughts and actions should
express our mind of compassion, even if that
person does and says things that are not easy
to accept. We practice in this way until we see
clearly that our love is not contingent upon the
other person being loveable.

THICH NHAT HANH

New eyes awaken.
I send Love's name into the world with wings.
THOMAS MERTON

• • • • •

To love at all is to be vulnerable.
Love anything, and your heart will certainly
be wrung and possibly broken.
C. S. LEWIS

Those who love deeply never grow old;
they may die of old age, but they die young.

Sir Arthur Pinero

· · · · ·

There is only one happiness in life,
to love and be loved.

George Sand

· · · · ·

When you do love a thing,
its gladness is a reason for loving it,
and its sadness a reason for loving it more.

G. K. Chesterton

Spread your love everywhere you go.

MOTHER TERESA

• • • • •

There is no remedy for love but to love more.

HENRY DAVID THOREAU

• • • • •

The little unremembered acts of kindness
and love are the best parts of a person's life.

WILLIAM WORDSWORTH

In moments of decision, we are to try to make what seems to be the most loving, the most creative decision. We are not to play safe, to draw back out of fear. Love may well lead us into danger. It may lead us to die for our friend. In a day when we are taught to look for easy solutions, it is not always easy to hold on to that most difficult one of all, love.

MADELEINE L'ENGLE

We need not think alike to love alike.

FRANCIS DAVID

• • • • •

Love is the only force capable
of transforming an enemy into friend.

MARTIN LUTHER KING JR.

Better is open rebuke than hidden love.

PROVERBS 27:5 NIV

• • • • •

*May the Lord make your love for each other
and for everyone else grow by leaps and bounds.
That's how our love for you has grown.*

1 THESSALONIANS 3:12 CEV

True love is that which ennobles the personality,
fortifies the heart, and sanctifies existence.

HENRI-FRÉDÉRIC AMIEL

• • • • •

True love suffers no concealment.

UNKNOWN

• • • • •

Love is to the moral nature exactly
what the sun is to the earth.

HONORÉ DE BALZAC

Love laughs at locksmiths.
UNKNOWN

• • • • •

To love is to be useful to yourself;
to cause love is to be useful to others.
PIERRE-JEAN DE BÉRANGER

• • • • •

Love is the true renewer.
ROGER DE BUSSY-RABUTIN

It is astonishing how little one feels poverty when one loves.

EDWARD GEORGE BULWER-LYTTON

Love doesn't grow on trees like apples in Eden—
it's something you have to make.
And you must use your imagination to make it, too,
just like anything else. It's all work, work.

JOYCE CARY

• • • • • •

Love is love's reward.

JOHN DRYDEN

A believing love will relieve us
of a vast load of care.

RALPH WALDO EMERSON

• • • • • •

Love concedes in a moment what we can
hardly attain by effort after years of toil.

JOHANN WOLFGANG VON GOETHE

• • • • • •

Love begins at home, and it is not how much we
do, but how much love we put into what we do.

MOTHER TERESA

Never self-possessed or prudent,
love is all abandonment.

RALPH WALDO EMERSON

• • • • •

We are shaped and fashioned
by what we love.

JOHANN WOLFGANG VON GOETHE

• • • • •

Those only obtain love,
for the most part, who seek it not.

JOHANN WOLFGANG VON GOETHE

The only way to understand [someone]
is to love her—and then it isn't necessary
to understand her.

SYDNEY HARRIS

• • • • •

Love, and you shall be loved.
All love is mathematically just, as much as
the two sides of an algebraic equation.

RALPH WALDO EMERSON

• • • • •

In love, all is risk.

JOHANN WOLFGANG VON GOETHE

Love understands love. It needs no talk.

SYDNEY HARRIS

• • • • •

The love we give away is the only love we keep.

ELBERT HUBBARD

• • • • •

When the mystery of God's love breaks through
into my consciousness, do I run from it?

KATHLEEN NORRIS

Love begets love.

LATIN PROVERB

Equality is the firmest bond of love.

GOTTHOLD EPHRAIM LESSING

• • • • •

Pure love cannot merely do all, but is all.

JEAN PAUL

• • • • •

Because we love, God is present.

THOMAS MERTON

Love consists in desiring to give
what is our own to another and
feeling his delight as our own.
EMANUEL SWEDENBORG

• • • • •

Love gives itself; it is not bought.
HENRY WADSWORTH LONGFELLOW

• • • • •

Love flies, runs, and rejoices;
it is free and nothing can hold it back.
THOMAS À KEMPIS

Paradise is always where

love dwells.

Jean Paul Richter

Convey love. . .as an arrow to the mark;
not as a ball against the wall,
to rebound back again.

FRANCIS QUARLES

• • • • •

From the beginning and to the end of the time,
Love reads without letters
and counts without arithmetic.

JOHN RUSKIN

Surprise us with love at daybreak;
then we'll skip and dance all the day long.
PSALM 90:14 MSG

• • • • •

The whole point of what we're urging is simply
love—love uncontaminated by self-interest and
counterfeit faith, a life open to God.
I TIMOTHY 1:5 MSG

Love is not love
which alters when it alteration finds.
WILLIAM SHAKESPEARE

• • • • •

Love covers a multitude of sins.
I PETER 4:8 NLT

• • • • •

We know that if we really want
to love, we must learn to forgive.
MOTHER TERESA

A [person] can be so changed by love as to be
unrecognizable as the same person.

TERENCE

• • • • •

Love looks not with the eyes, but with the mind.

WILLIAM SHAKESPEARE

• • • • •

Love conquers all the world,
let us, too, yield to love.

VIRGIL

Love betters what is best.

WILLIAM WORDSWORTH

• • • • •

Love is, above all, the gift of oneself.

JEAN ANOUILH

• • • • •

To be grateful is to recognize the love of God
in everything He has given us.

THOMAS MERTON

Love is the heart's immortal thirst to be
completely known and all forgiven.

HENRY VAN DYKE

• • • • •

They do not love, that do not show their love.

WILLIAM SHAKESPEARE

• • • • •

Love is the master key that opens
the gates of happiness.

OLIVER WENDELL HOLMES

It doesn't matter how long we may have been stuck in a sense of our limitations. If we go into a darkened room and turn on the light, it doesn't matter if the room has been dark for a day or a week or ten thousand years—we turn on the light, and it is illumined. Once we contact our capacity for love and happiness. . .the light has been turned on.

SHARON SALZBERG

Love should run out to meet love with open arms.
ROBERT LEWIS STEVENSON

. . . . .

Finally, we are as we love.
It is love that measures our stature.
WILLIAM SLOANE COFFIN

. . . . .

Love. . .is perhaps the only glimpse
we are permitted of eternity.
HELEN HAYES

Love alone is capable of uniting human beings
in such a way as to complete and fulfill them,
for it alone takes them and joins them
by what is deepest in themselves.

PIERRE TEILHARD DE CHARDIN

• • • • • •

Love is difficult. For one human being to love
another is perhaps the most difficult task of all,
the epitome, the ultimate test. It is that striving for
which all other striving is merely preparation.

RAINIER MARIE RILKE

That is true love which always and forever remains the same, whether one grants it everything or denies it everything.

JOHANN WOLFGANG VON GOETHE

• • • • •

To love is the great amulet that makes this world a garden.

ROBERT LOUIS STEVENSON

• • •

No cord or cable can draw so forcibly, or bind so fast, as love can do with a single thread.

ROBERT BURTON

Love must be learned, and learned again,
and again; there is no end to it.

KATHERINE ANN PORTER

• • • • •

Nothing is sweeter than love,
nothing more courageous, nothing higher,
nothing wider, nothing more pleasant,
nothing fuller nor better in heaven and earth;
because love is born of God,
and cannot rest but in God,
above all created things.

THOMAS À KEMPIS

The countless generations
Like autumn leaves go by;
Love only is eternal,
Love only does not die.

HARRY KEMP

All love is sweet,
Given or returned.
PERCY BYSSHE SHELLEY

• • • • •

The giving of love is an education in itself.
ELEANOR ROOSEVELT.

Love and compassion are
necessities, not luxuries.
Without them, humanity cannot survive.

TENZIN GYATSO

• • • • •

Love is the best friend of humankind,
the helper and the healer of all ills
that stand in the way of human happiness.

PLATO

• • • • •

Love is the scope of all God's commands.

JOHN CHRYSOSTOM

What does love look like?
It has hands to help others.
It has feet to hasten to the poor and needy.
It has eyes to see misery and want.
It has ears to hear the sighs
and sorrows of humankind.
That is what love looks like.

SAINT AUGUSTINE

Let's see how inventive we can be in encouraging love and helping out, not avoiding worshiping together as some do but spurring each other on.

<small>HEBREWS 10:24 MSG</small>

· · · · · ·

Give thanks to the Lord, for he is good! His faithful love endures forever.

<small>PSALM 106:1 NLT</small>

He does much who loves God much.

THOMAS À KEMPIS

• • • • •

You live that you may learn to love,
you love that you may learn to live.

MIRDAD

• • • • •

He alone is great who turns the voice
of the wind into a song made sweeter
by his own loving.

KHALIL GIBRAN

It is love that fashions us
into the fullness of our being—not our looks,
not our work, not our wants,
not our achievements, not our parents,
not our status, not our dreams.
These are all the fodder and the filler,
the navigating fuels of our lives; but it is love:
who we love, how we love,
why we love, and that we love,
which ultimately shapes us.

DAPHNE ROSE KINGMA

Love courses through everything.
No, Love *is* everything.
How can you say there is no love,
when nothing but love exists?
All that you see has appeared
because of Love.
All shines from Love.
All pulses from Love.
All flows from Love.
No, once again, all *is* Love.

Araqi

It is in the shelter of each other that people live.

IRISH PROVERB

• • • • •

Love is a choice.
Not simply, or necessarily,
a rational choice,
but rather a willingness to be
present to others without pretence or guile.

CARTER HEYWARD

It is not the perfect but the imperfect
that have need of love.

OSCAR WILDE

• • • • •

In the gentle relief of another's care,
In the darkness of night and the winter's snow,
In the naked and outcast,
Seek love there.

WILLIAM BLAKE

May it be, oh Lord,
that I seek not so much to be
consoled as to console,
to be understood as to understand,
to be loved as to love.
Because it is in giving oneself
that one receives;
it is in forgetting oneself
that one is found.

FRANCIS OF ASSISI

One of the deepest secrets of life
is that all that is really worth doing
is what we do for others.

Lewis Carroll

• • • • •

If we have loved well while we were alive,
there is life after death here—
our love will go on for generations.

Desmond Tutu

If I can stop one heart from breaking,
I shall not live in vain;
If I can ease one life the aching,
Or cool one pain
Or help one fainting robin
Unto his nest again,
I shall not live in vain.

EMILY DICKINSON

In the end, nothing we do or say in this lifetime will matter as much as the way we have loved one another.

DAPHNE ROSE KINGMA

• • • • •

God's love, God's voice and presence, would instill our souls with such affirmation we would need nothing more and would cause us to love other people so much we would be willing to die for them.

DONALD MILLER

Knowing is the most
profound kind of love,
giving someone the gift of
knowledge about yourself.

MARSHA NORMAN

I am done with great things and big plans,
great institutions and big success.
I am for those tiny, invisible, loving human
forces that work from individual to individual,
creeping through the crannies of the world
like so many rootlets, or like the capillary
oozing of water, which if given time,
will rend the hardest monuments of pride.

WILLIAM JAMES

• • • • •

If you would be loved, love and be loveable.

BENJAMIN FRANKLIN

Don't run up debts, except for the huge debt of love you owe each other. When you love others, you complete what the law has been after all along. The law code—don't sleep with another person's spouse, don't take someone's life, don't take what isn't yours, don't always be wanting what you don't have, and any other "don't" you can think of—finally adds up to this: Love other people as well as you do yourself. You can't go wrong when you love others. When you add up everything in the law code, the sum total is love.

ROMANS 13:8–10 MSG

It is not love, but lack of love, which is blind.

GLENWAY WESTCOTT

• • • • •

Love is always open arms. If you close your arms
around love, you will find that
you are left holding only yourself.

LEO BUSCAGLIA

• • • • •

We don't love qualities, we love a person;
sometimes by reason of their defects
as well as their qualities.

JACQUES MARITAIN

Love opens the door into everything,
as far as I can see, including, and perhaps
most of all, the door into one's own secret,
and often terrible and frightening, real self.

MAY SARTON

● ● ● ● ●

Trouble is a part of life, and if you don't share
it, you don't give the person who loves you a
chance to love you enough.

DINAH SHORE

Love is something you and I must have.
We must have it because our spirit feeds upon
it. We must have it because without
it we become weak and faint.
Without love our self-esteem weakens.
Without it our courage fails.
Without love we can no longer look
confidently at the world. . . .
With it, and with it alone,
we are able to sacrifice for others.

DAN GEORGE

The real prizes were not. . .
health, wealth, and happiness. . .which could
be destroyed so easily by the first breath of
misfortune, but faith, hope,
and, above all, love.

SUSAN HOWATCH

Love is a short word, but it contains it all:
it means the body, the soul, the life,
the entire being. We felt it as we feel the warmth
of the blood, we breathe it as we breathe the air,
we carry it in ourselves as we carry our
thoughts. Nothing more exists for us.
It is not a word; it is an inexpressible state
indicated by four letters.

GUY DE MAUPASSANT

Love gives courage to the most fearful;
sharpens the wit of the most simple; . . .
[gives] constancy to the most unsettled;
and, of itself alone, hath power to draw
those hearts which have received it
to acts of goodness, honesty, virtue. . . .
None are made happy without love.

ALGERNON SIDNEY

• • • • •

Above all, love each other deeply,
because love covers over a multitude of sins.

1 PETER 4:8 NIV

[Love] is a fire that, kindling its first embers in the narrow nook of the private bosom, caught from a wandering spark out of another private heart, glows and enlarges until it warms and beams upon multitudes of men and women. . .and so lights up the whole world and all nature with its flames.

RALPH WALDO EMERSON

When I felt my feet slipping,
you came with your love
and kept me steady.

PSALM 94:18 CEV

Our job is to love others without stopping
to inquire whether or not they are worthy.
That is not our business and, in fact,
it is nobody's business. What we are asked to do
is to love, and this love itself will render both
ourselves and our neighbors worthy.

THOMAS MERTON

• • • • •

Works of love are always works of peace.

MOTHER TERESA

Love is *part* of the answer, sure, but just part.
Hope is another part, and courage,
and charity, and laughter, and really *seeing*
things like how green pine trees look after
a rain, and how the setting sun can turn
a prairie into molten gold glass.

DEAN KOONTZ

• • • • •

To trust Abba, both in prayer and life,
is to stand in childlike openness before a
mystery of gracious love and acceptance.

BRENNAN MANNING

Were the whole realm
of nature mine,
That were a present far too small:
Love so amazing, so divine,
Demands my soul, my life, my all.

ISAAC WATTS

Really, all authentic Christian spiritual practices
are practices of one thing: love. Love for God.
Love for the other—the neighbor,
the enemy, the last, the least, the lost.
So our basic practice is to love each other.

BRIAN MCLAREN

* * * * *

Love is a fruit always in season,
and no limit is set.
Everyone can reach this love.

MOTHER TERESA